Spillway

Spillway

volume 2, issue 30

guest edited by
torrin a. greathouse & Rachel McKibbens

MOON
TIDE PRESS

~ 2024 ~

Spillway: volume 2, issue 30

Editor-in-chief
Eric Morago

***Spillway* Managing Editor**
Ellen Webre

Guest Editors
torrin a. greathouse & Rachel McKibbens

Associate Editor
Shelly Holder

Proofreader
Elaine Mintzer

Front cover art
Amanda Le

Book design
Michael Wada

Moon Tide logo design
Abraham Gomez

Spillway: volume 2, issue 30
is published by Moon Tide Press

Moon Tide Press
6709 Washington Ave. #9297
Whittier, CA 90608
www.moontidepress.com

FIRST EDITION

Printed in the United States of America

ISBN #978-1-957799-16-2

Contents

Tamara Zbrizher
In line at the Wawa   101

Foreword

A teacher gives a student a glass of water and tells the student to dance. The student goes and dances and, after a few minutes, comes back to the teacher and says "It's hard to dance without spilling the water." The teacher laughs and says "Who said that you shouldn't spill the water?"

When Eric Morago asked me to be *Spillway Magazine*'s new managing editor, I was excited and daunted. While I had had experience editing for my college literary magazine and *FreezeRay*, this would be my first time ever being a managing editor. *Spillway Magazine* has been around since 1996, sharing beautiful pieces of writing and art and was a yearly cornerstone of Mifanwy Kaiser's Tebot Bach's publications—their final issue's guest editors were the illustrious Lynne Thompson and Patricia Smith. I am so honored to be able to continue Mifanwy's legacy and hope to do the magazine justice as its new managing editor.

Moon Tide Press's goal has always been to celebrate necessary voices whose works are imaginative, honest, and engaging. I immediately knew I wanted Rachel McKibbens and torrin a. greathouse to be our first guest editors, because I believe in their writing and trust their taste. Rachel and torrin have the consistent ability to pierce my heart with the beauty and brutality of their words, and I knew that they would choose heartfelt pieces to move the spirit.

In this volume, you will find exploration of grief, love, and the strength that endures beyond wounding. The book cover, beautifully illustrated by Amanda Le, intends to depict the spirit of this volume. Many thanks to all our collaborators for their hard work and dedication. Many thanks to every single person who submitted to this journal. And, of course, thank you to Mifanwy and Tebot Bach for entrusting Moon Tide with *Spillway*; we promise to build on its past greatness and carry it far into the future.

To make art is to move and feel deeply. To share it is proof of life spilling onto the page like water in a dancer's cup. We are so grateful to be able to share these works with you in *Spillway Magazine #30* and look forward to sharing many more. We hope you will enjoy this collection and find inspiration in these pages.

With best regards,
Ellen Webre
Managing Editor
Spillway Magazine

Ritual for Moving

I open the porch door,
shake loose a rough night
in the rush of cool.

In my kitchen,
a pillow cradles my back.
I wait at the table
for something
to make me
want to move.

I look up at the old clock,
note the time left
before I have to be
somewhere else.

After she died,
it was strange
having time.
It's taken
some years
to fill it.

Now, I look for magic
in the uncharted hours:
scrubbing tiles
ironing a vest
folding socks
washing dishes

looking out the window.

Dania Ayah Alkhouli

M is for Maskoon

adverb from the Arabic root word 'sakan' or an abode of found tranquility; translates to occupied house. Colloquially, it's come to be known as a house possessed (by a spirit).

It's 1:23 a.m. and I undress another haunted house
before the mirror; blushing peach fields
spilling from the midnight denim of the night.

When your black eyes opened up this house,
appraised my flesh and found creaking foundations
you can't tiptoe around without getting caught—
you asked what man wants a woman like that.

So instead, those ashy hands dug a grave beneath
my chest; that sharp tongue slowly slit the epitaph
across a throat already choked with shattered grief.

You clawed your way between my thighs and left
behind the dirt of women before me, stuck
underneath your fingernails; now traces
of a woman—whose name you can't remember—

live inside me. Flakes of white
girl merging inside this body
everyone still keeps trying to paint white.

A sisterhood now brews within me.
Footsteps pulsating at the turquoise of my veins.
Every woman you lost behind becomes found in me.
So I tell myself I am sacred now.

A home of scars—a house
haunted.

Robin Axworthy

The Night I Didn't Listen

"I haven't any anesthetic...her screams are not important."

— Ernest Hemingway

It wasn't until night milking that we saw the skin
hanging down from her bag just over her left teat—
probably caught on a piece of scrap metal
we'd never gotten around to putting away—

my dear Nubian goat with her long ears,
her coat tender as fawns, her ancient eyes,
gold and slit. Her crusted teats soft
in my hands, the sound of her milk,
its sharp scent as it drilled
into the bucket between my knees.

I wanted to call the vet.
We don't have the money you said.
Yes. We were two dirt-poor hippies trying
to farm. *We can do it ourselves*, you said—
like you thought you could officiate marriages,
change the town council with your arguments,
like you'd built your own house. And I'd grown up
watching Dad stitch animals closed all my life.

I stiffened myself, agreed.

I held her head tight while you punched
the sterilized rug needle through barrier of skin
with your pliers, knotted the button thread, repeated.

She fought. We tied her back legs so she couldn't kick.

Why didn't I feel how a breast hurts?

You kept stitching, a kind of desperate effort.
And then suddenly she was gone,
her knees buckling to the hay.

We tried, you said. Shrugged. *How were we to know?* —
washing your hands of it. I looked at you
in the light of the 40-watt bulb, her body, your boots,
my ears still ringing. I couldn't hear your words,

only her harsh bellows and the silence,
still falling.

Kay E. Bancroft

Test Seat

each leg strapped in by supple leather and we grasp for new skin,
we feel the blood rush through our reddened necks. glance at
our thighs — in the tighter bends each fold of us unfurling
our limbs pulse against cold crevasse as onlookers move past
silver scuffed by rings, the spectacle. we pick our
fingernails, repeat the motion of working cuticles off to distract from failure to mold
curves of our bodies into restraints — us. somehow we forget to realize that,
if we were home, this could be pleasurable. in their eyes, we did this to ourselves.
we might enjoy it more if strangers would not gawk, squeal, grumble, and pass
witness as we shimmy our thighs like this shame beneath the breath, low in the lungs —
heave, groan, fresh craving for what? a consolation, a balm
for silence when the body screams out for each fear manifested
for others, for ourselves in the spectacle.

Wound Botany

Late-winter wind howls through maple branches
outside my window, and so do I. By this, I mean my
body, too, may rip through clusters of vermillion buds,
create its own botany, whistle its way down.
Not literally, of course — or, maybe a small branch impales
my palm. Buds surround the wound made from myself,
the tree's bark. Somehow, we've become one, meshed irregular
biologies for the first time. I examine the wound; rough edged,
porous, and pulsing. I think this is how I feel about
being perceived as any gender. Something struck through
me against my will — I am forced to feel around it. Maneuver
softness of my wounds around terms unsuitable, illegally lodged.
I'd like to wrench them away, but I've been told that when impaled
it's safest to leave the weapons inside. Even if it kills you.

[What Follows] in the Blood

Lending unfamiliar shape to itself
once again, [ ] breaks
a window with [ ]' tongue. Throws
human-like body through glass' once-
home — a cortex of crystal, hexagonal
light. [ ] hears the tremble in this girl's
breath. Vibration lingering in chasmic
pseudo ears shaped like those she might know.
This girl *needs* to know if this not-man across
from her sees [ ] in the house, begs
to check the eating room. He perceives nothing

but space. Sticky

linoleum, broken

candlestick, receiver

nestles a

phone. No

one. No

body. No

raisin teeth rearing heads from the sanctum
of a mouth. One breast pillowed in stale air, swinging
across crumpled valley of an underwire bra, pleading for touch.
[ ]' midriff is cold, barren between fields of stained cotton and
piss-
soaked athletic skirt. [ ] drags its feet —

one naked,

other cloaked

in a tube sock, curating a paced
slap/thud/slap/thud/slap/thud.

What curdles across them?

this girl paints the territory in her throat's native tongue —
perceiving what was dedicated to her.

No

consent, only

privilege to

carry the wound,

open-faced like her

thighs in the backseat of

a vintage coupe, no

knowledge of

her body's reception,

of what pulses under luminescent skin,

opaline origin known,

jilted.

What follows all in her

line until it transfers.

Until it passes from her

wound to the next.
Until they die.

All of them.

Lyra Bateman

Gonna Get Me

Mary Beth Becker

Fire Season
after Kate Daniels

When I think of the smoke rolling in like horsemen
from the west, the sequoias invisible in the thickness
of carbon and flame, when I think of the doe, the twin fawns
and their legs buckling, their lungs charred and exhausted
and their young spotted backs gray now with ash, I think
of their habitual silence changed to a thin keening, the wet
of their charcoal noses dry now and unexceptional,
I think of what they saw last, was it bruise-yellow, was it
one spruce colliding with another, or instead the taste,
not the sight of the burning? And when I think of the burning,
I think of the sun's fever down on low tide, the mollusks
cooked to death in their shells, their little sacs of flesh
popped open and the sound they made, and could they
hear one another, I think of the oysters rotting open
to the sky, barnacles dissolved into salt, sea stars
shriveling to zero on the shore, I think of the flesh
on that beach in Vancouver, the fish-rot and calamity,
and when I think of calamity I think of the albatross
and the avocet and their bellies full of bottlecap, I think
of their eggs, their speckled eggs laid four at a time
for luck, the life in them hard-boiling, I think
of the mothers, waiting and warming and nothing
coming of it, no flight, no thing, I try not to think of
the future, the great plastic nation assembling
out there, in the sea, when I think of the future
there is only this present, only the downed trees
and the dead birds and the horizon, blotted out with smoke.

Hummingbirds

In the morning
I drove to the grocery store
and all day
I thought about the car
parked next to me
when I came out
arms full of produce
the sticker on the rear window
said *God bless our troops,*
especially our snipers.

It was no longer enough
to go about my day
feeding the cat
watering the plants
refilling the bird feeder
looking out the window
while I worked, hoping to see
the flash of a hummingbird
a fleeting green spark
like the way we imagine
all life begins.

Blue Light

As a girl, I sat on the icy tile
studied Father's flick of straight

razor, sharp scissors, learned
the danger of a leading edge. I

poured the blue light of Aqua Velva
into his cupped palm, inhaled swill

of alcohol, mint, and musk.
I bore witness to his ministration

as he punished ruddy cheeks
with—double-slap,

hard lean to glass. Toothy wand
dragged through dense black

curls, pomade slick—a ritual
of vainglory for a leading man.

This is where beauty
began and ended in our house.

He wanted me to watch
because without my wide-eyed

adulation—his artistry unfinished,
the film forever uncut.

The Appointment

The surgeon says the cancer
on my father's earlobe is easy
to remove, no more effort
than pitting a cherry, but my father,
who is a slick 80-year-old
with Al Pacino looks,
Godfather demeanor, warns
Boy, don't' take too much.

I sit a silent witness when
the surgeon punctures the lobe
with a hypodermic of numbing
medication, scalpels a slit, then
another, excavates a hole
the size of a Buffalo nickel.
Soon, stitches stammer
over the intertragic notch,

remains of my father's lobe
connecting to the stubble
on his cheek, skin flushed
to a pomegranate red, blood
in the orbit of the ear.
My father tries to inspect
the mutilation with his thumb

and forefinger, but instead, fumbles
along the ridgeline of his jaw.
Take a damn picture with your phone,
he commands. I do as I'm told.

Alexandra Burack

Memory of the Country
after Cavafy

Coral double peonies recline
over chipped and purplish lips
of the market-stall vase we saved
to embellish our meager farmhouse
table, blushed in its shroud of candlelight.
Your last night in undomesticated rooms,
and I feel your flight already to the border
of the unkempt field amid relics
from the last war, dented underground
for treasure hunters to scavenge.
The border of your heart now mapless.
Will you remember the respiring
garden and how petals brushed
our ears to better spill their stories,
then knew with the indifference
of flowers how life bourgeons
and in the arc of its fullness,
is spent?

On Hungerford Bridge

Underneath, the Thames churls in velvet
brown: burnished-brass river roiling
its alchemy almost into gold,
giving up perfect circles of foam
which seem whispers of jaundiced smoke.

The abandoned woman contemplates her leap,
a ricochet of longing. On the footpath,
canals of soil-stained puddles the drains
can't carry down, so there is no surface
where water does not draw her. Trains thunder-

roll, the walkway shudders. Imagine
the pavement split, the stride onto air. She walks
into this possibility, recalls another stateless
one gone missing. December, midnight, asleep
on a train stalled above water, failed signal ahead.

Lurched out of a dream by the conductor's tin
voice. *My stop*, she gasped, leapt up, pried the door,
trundled into nothing. The river released
her body in Spring, when there was no more face
for the story of that irretrievable step.

Jessica June Cato

Avoiding the Truth with My Therapist

I'm trying to tell you those billionaires were taken out by orcas. Mermaids hired them, sick of the microplastics. Can you be a little more specific? My therapist is trying to redirect me again. Let me start over. Water is sacred, right? Showers, bathes, rain after drought. Baptisms. I didn't know I was baptized until my twenties. My stepmom laughed when she told me. I can't help but feel the orcas wouldn't respect that move. I'm going to probe you a little bit here. I want to tell my therapist that I'm pulling my eyelashes again, but I tell her I don't think the bowl of water saved my soul nor did the frilly white dress, or the creepy guy in a different dress dunking my bald head. I was bald until I was two. I was a bald, and verbose baby. Do you think the orcas near Europe are teaching their babies how to capsize yachts? They should, all little things should be taught to defend what they love, defend themselves. Maybe there's a finite amount of love, maybe some people simply get less. I challenge that. She's trying to get me to talk about my friend who stumbled away before the ambulance arrived. If he had been addicted to water, I wouldn't have to write poems about him. But that means my venom bubbles upward like the submarine. Did you know it's actually not a submarine, technically it's a submersible. Submarines can free themselves from the depths, submersibles cannot.

Sarah ChristianScher

The Folly of De-evolution

You'll find that moving your nostrils
to the top of your head is easier
than going from lungs to gills.
Arches long since repurposed
turned to: jaw, larynx,
tiny bones nestled in the ear.
Going back means losing so much.
This is all to say I have evolved past
the point at which I could ever come
back to you.

Vanity

I stole my mother's 14K gold horse charm with emerald eyes before she died. Freed it from her charm bracelet, put it on a delicate chain around my neck, tucked in close to my heart. Then it disappeared. Never recovered. The horse charm. My beautiful mother. *You see*, she'd taunt. *You're not to be trusted with precious things!* Each day I'd watch her transformation at the dressing room vanity: moisturizer, primer, medium beige base coat, blended under chin, down her neck; smoothed into décolletage. Then rouge, liner, brows brushed and darkened. Two coats of Maybelline Blackest Black Mascara. A generous swipe of Revlon's Fire & Ice lipstick. After my mother died, I kept the tiny tub of green liner I found in her makeup drawer - decades later - finger the expired pigment, rub it over my eyelids, like she used to. But I am not so enigmatic. She often told me I could never compare. Still, I dip the tiny brush into water, then the dazzling hue, outline my dark brown eyes. The result is startling: green makes my eyes "pop" as my mother used to say. But then her ghost is over my shoulder, staring at my reflection. Something's missing. She shakes her head. Sidles up to my ear. *Looking for this?* My mother opens her left hand; the horse charm glistens, emerald eyes dancing in the light. Like her love, she holds it just out of my reach.

Lauren Frost

goldilocks depression

the girl in the bed is the second offense of the morning. first: how
did the porridge i made come out three different temperatures?
i can't cook, can't clean, everything spoiled. my aggressive family
off in a huff when i fail their expectations. i take a shortcut
through glossy bushes and glittering trees, trying to remember i'm
alive in a fairytale. then i am earliest back. earliest to find

the girl in the bed, who says, i am like you. i also feel too much
or too little, and which is worse? either i'm breaking down doors,
smashing up chairs, or i'm never leaving my slice of the forest
at all? i cup her chin in my claws. she has unremarkable hair,
yellowed by dirt. don't make me get up, she says. i am the
exact right amount of sad.

double decker

i am unshowered and unemployed and
      halfway under a seventeen-hour greyhound
to my friend phil's new year's eve rager
      when phil texts that party's off, phil's roommate
woke up to bed bugs drinking his feet
      so now they've stuck their whole apartment in
the laundromat. i still ride all the way

to port authority, where we let out in a
      clammed up basement terminal and i decrunch
twelve dollars for a devastating sub
      sandwich because i can't be bothered to have fun
in new cities anymore. then it's back on

the greyhound, plus this one's sold out so
      i'm flush against a fellow out-of-stater watching
finding nemo full burst on an iphone.
      he's got no earbuds, it's three a-m, i'm humming
on half a night of bus dreams and a sub
      that was mostly bread. please, can you turn
the sound down? no thanks, he says.

happy twenty-nineteen: nemo is located
      and i blubber on the interstate like a damn song,
but i've never believed the beginning
      of a year means anything more than a bug
in the washer, killed by the cycle.

Chameleon's Threnody or Woman & a Pint of Ice Cream on a Friday Night

"Best day ever!"

—Jeff Bezos

I count backwards   galaxy   lift off   hoping humanity
comes to its senses and starts feeding its own Black & Brown babies
instead of comparing whose rocket is largest—
elite touring stars, colonizing even space.

But I digress. I'm wrapped in a blanket on my sofa
crying in my chocolate chip cookie dough.
Before you roll your eyes at me and release *dramatic*
from under your breath, recall that I, too,
have an environmental vision
where people who look like me are freed from
a society that merely tolerates us.

My neighbor comments to my husband,
Black people have it pretty good.
Because he, of course, is white
and because my husband, too,
is white,
carrying on the unspoken agreement.

Around here, we set-up our security surveillance
before we wave our Black Lives Matter flag.
Because racists believe in the right to free speech
only when it's convenient.
And then there are the racists that are so nice to me
that make me second guess their racism.
I have to remind myself that the dismissal of basic human rights
is normalized white supremacy.

There are also those that don't hold other white people
accountable.
Every time you ignore injustice a bell rings
and a brown girl loses her wings.

By now my ice cream is a puddle of melt and salt and
I'm no longer interested in the taste.
I count backwards. You can't distract me.

I see you and real recognizes real:
true change is carried in the heart,
with compassion.
With grace.
Don't make me launch into space and find you.

No Small Happiness

To imagine the earth will go on
without us, brings me no small

happiness. And with little faith
in God, modest comfort to believe

I might escape further judgement.
After all, what would either of us

have to say? Even as my son
hugs me good-bye this morning,

I know the ways I've failed him —
how we all keep failing, the planet's

inheritance already squandered.
They say all a man has in the end

are his memories. But I won't take
even these into oblivion. No need

for an afterlife, endless time to climb
the same regretful stairs, reliving

a life I've shoved like a grand piano
into a room too small to hold it.

Such a pleasure to know I'll be gone.
Whittled away to nothing, and yet

still crawling in whatever low creature
survives in this world to crawl:

cockroach and silverfish, the simple ant.
Why does it bring me such peace,

this notion of disappearing? To know
when Jesus spoke of the meek,

He didn't mean us.

Dirgelings

a found poem of species lost due to human activity

Arabian ostrich / Ascension crake / Atlas wild ass / Aurochs /
Atlas bear / Big-eared hopping mouse / Bluebuck / Bramble Cay
melomys / Broad-billed parrot / Bubal hartebeest / Bulldog rat /
Bushwren / California grizzly bear / Canary Islands oystercatcher /
Cape lion / Caribbean monk seal / Caroline parakeet / Carpathian
wisent / Caucasian wisent / Cebu warty pig / Chadwick Beachcotton
mouse / Chatham bellbird / Chatham fernbird / Colombian grebe /
Colpocephalum californici / Cuban macaw / Delalande's coua / Dodo
/ Domed Mauritius giant tortoise / Domed Rodrigues giant tortoise
/ Dusky seaside sparrow / Eastern elk / Eiao monarch / Epioblasma
haysiana / Erica warhami / Felicola isidoroi / Formosan clouded
leopard / Goff's pocket gopher / Gravenche / Great auk / Guam
flying fox / Gull Island vole / Haast's eagle / Heath hen / Hemigrapsus
estellinensis / Huia / Japanese Otter / Japanese seal lion / Kangaroo
Island emu / King Island emu / Laughing owl / Lesser moa / Lyall's
wren / Macquarie parakeet / Madeiran scops owl / Malagasy crowned
eagle / Martinique amazon / Mauritius blue pigeon / Mauritius scops
owl / Merriam's elk / Moa / Mount Glorious day frog / Nesoryzomys
darwini / Nesoryzomys indefessus / New Zealand greater short-tailed
bat / New Zealand musk duck / New Zealand owlet-nightjar / New
Zealand quail/ Newton's parakeet / Norfolk kākā / Noronhomys
/ North Island giant moa / North Island snipe / O'ahu nukupu'u
/ O'ahu 'ōʻō / O'ahu 'akialoa / Oryzomys antillarum / Pantanodon
madagascariensis / Paschalococos / Passenger pigeon / Piopio /
Quagga / Ratas Island lizard / Réunion giant tortoise / Robust crow
/ Rocky Mountain locust / Round Island burrowing boa / St. Croix
macaw / San Marcos gambusia / San Martin Island woodrat / São
Miguel scops owl / Schomburgk's deer / Sea mink / Small Mauritian
flying fox / South Island snipe / South Island stout-legged wren /
Southern black rhinoceros / Steller's sea cow / Syncaris pasadenae /

Syrian elephant / Syrian wild ass / Tarpan / Tasmania em**u** / Tecopa pupfish / Thicktail chub / Thismia americana / Javan tiger / Tool**ache** wallaby / Tristramella intermedia / Upland moa / Wake Island rail / Western black **r**hinoceros / Western Lewin's rail / Xerces blue

```
        stri   /                ke /                  /  u      s /
           /                        /                /
           /                        /                /              /
           /     f r                /                o              /
           /          m             /                /        th
      e /                /          r      /              e   co
           /              rd /   h              / ol              /
                    /                    / D              u /
   /         s      to     /
   /     y              o /              /              /
           /                        /              /                u
      r /                        / Grave      / G          /
        o /          n    e / H   ea   /              /        r
   t    s /          /                  /                  / K
      e /                    e  /                  /              /
              p         /                  o  /
      /          u        /        r        /
      /                /    /                  / N
   a     /          m    e s   / Ne     a     r
           and              /                let              /
   al        l/     t                  /              /        h
   /     Is            mo  /                  /    u
   /         /                  /  r                  /    n
           i n   /                  /     g    g o  /                  /
      a /    s    a        d / Ré      a                  /
   /     M                  / R                  /
       /                  /                  /
      e          /     m        e /    m   /
       /                  /                  /
       b         er  /                  / S                  /
           /                  /    /                  u /
```

```
       s /              /              /          /    ache
w      /  i t        t      /        /                   /
           hi        /    t               /
```

Clearing

We are both ourselves and the trees.

—Katie Holten, 'Deciphering Words in the Woods',
Emergence Magazine, 20 November 2020

If I think about it too much
I can forget what it feels like
        to be a clearance:
to have a body   that is disappearing
bit by covert bit,
unable to point to any specific trunk or limb
and say
it was here
it was meant   to be here
why is it   not here?

If I strain,   I can subtle   the thinning   of spirit
like a book   where all the letters fade
        and you read   by their serifs
instead;
meaning   cobbled   in detritus,
        terminal edges   not yet vanished
gathered   for scraps.

    If I want,   I can ignore   how
    I am   unlanguaged,
how the mind   comes to be
bone-cracked
        timber,
why dreams   loosen   like
soil
and   become
diaspora   to the slept.

        I don't have to feel   this
taproot,

                         this hand,
                              this child's hungry mouth

flexing for something   to root in,

                                        grasp for,
                                        latch onto

     amidst that   deep,

                                        dark
                                        nothing
               of soil

     that has

                                        become
                                        a
                              self.
                         but

m   ay   be
                                                                          I
          sho   ul   d
s   t
o   p   t   o
    fe

     e   l   b   e
          f   o
re
          I

     d   i   s

                         a   p   p

     e   a   r
c   o   m

40

p   l

e   t   e

        l

41

How I Made Myself a Sexist Trope: A Manual

For months, I dreamed of my face
looking up from a car trunk,
mottled throat in the bruise prints
of my ex's hands.

I put my body in a trunk
night after night,
tucked myself under a little death
for warmth.

In daytime, asthma provided the previews
for the midnight screenings.
A cough, a pressure, a little choking
to set the mood.

Thumbed the picture
of my daughter's bruised forearms.
Remembered the strength of his hands,
the weight of his body above mine.

I made myself airless and still,
smaller and smaller to fit a box.
I'd always regretted the space I take,
the volume of my voice, its breaking.

So, yes, I'd found relief in its silencing,
worshipped the ideal of perfect victim,
drafted my daily obituary:
So sweet and kind, so quiet, so good.

I lit candles for myself,
perfected a stillborn future
and feigned innocence
until my daughter's logic sliced my veil

You aren't important enough to him
*   to harm.*

When You Find the Tiger You Escaped Living inside the Cage of Your Ribs
A Cento of Self-Harm *

How the hell are we supposed to live
believing in man. Believing in tiger.

They could do *to* you all day long,
and you could just not-be.
There's only so much goodness
one body can hold.
On this side—flesh; on that—
an iron claw.
Are you broke, or broken?

Always good to trade one thing for another—
taking bones for diamonds.
Strike that. Stroke again.
You are finally being punished.
Disaster in thick gauze
of happiness.

Strong wrists that can pin and twist
yourself. The difference
between mere torture and true humiliation
moves back and forth to a song
of no mercy.

What is a song if no one will sing it
to the touch.
Every muscle has a name.
It is all coming back around—
the best hurt they'll ever know
was in the participation
of the victim.

What did I need with Hell now
I could feel you behind my eyes
with the lunge and growl of a tiger.
Between the stripes
are what we've made of ourselves.
You can't stop smiling
of tiger.
How hard it is
not to be the tiger.

You've been broken in.
You cannot think of a time
you have ever been happier.

*"When You Find the Tiger You Escaped Living inside Your Ribs:
A Cento of Self-Harm" incorporates lines from the following
poems, novels or podcasts:

- Brendan Constantine, "Inquisition" *Birthday Girl with Possum;*
- Tanya Olson "How Hard It Is to Not Buy a Tiger" *Boyishly;*
- Lois McMaster Bujold, *Mirror Dance;*
- Keetje Kuipers, "Bondage Play as Substitution for Prayer"
  Beautiful in the Mouth;
- Saeed Jones "Prelude to Bruise" *Prelude to Bruise;*
- Jan Beatty "Hitchhike" *Red Sugar;*
- Aracelis Girmay "Dear Minnie, Dear Ms." *Kingdom Animalia;*
- Tracy K. Smith "Studio" *The Body's Question;*
- *Welcome to Night Vale,* Episode 13 "A Story about You";
- Sonia Greenfield "Conquistadors" *Boy with a Halo at the
  Farmer's Market;*
- Danez Smith "From My Window" *[Insert Boy];*
- Gabrielle Calvocoressi "Training Camp: Deer Lake, PA"
  Apocalyptic Swing;
- Kaveh Akbar "An Apology" *Calling A Wolf A Wolf;*
- Donika Kelly "Love Poem: Chimera" *Bestiary;*
- Mary Jo Bang "A Calculation Based on Figures in a Scene"
  The Last Two Seconds.

4th Street and Grand Avenue

On the corner of la cuatro and Grand,
where sex workers sought employment,
stood la Iglesia de Nuestra Señora de Guadalupe.
A porcelain Mary, taller and paler than the real one,
endured outside
protected by metal bars and a moat of cacti.

Down la cuatro,
the trees were decorated in graffiti.
I took this street to misa
where they sold bibles
and bottles of holy salt water
that abuelas bought with rattling copper.

South of Grand was where I fell for a believer—
a Gemini who sipped ginseng tea
and wore a plastic rosary.
For Christmas, I gave her a stolen ring
made of blue cubic zirconia laid into a cross.
She said I was a Virgo, and we were too different.

Thames

Thames smiles at me after he makes the shadows.
"Can you see the bear?"
"the goat?"
"the face?"

Thames is in the fifth grade. He's smart - all his teachers say so.

He remembered all 50 states: Delaware, North Dakota, South
Dakota, Minnesota, Wyoming and
the rest. He even remembered all the capitals: Dover, Bismarck,
Pierre, Saint Paul, Cheyenne and all the others.

Thames said the trick is to remember the capitals with the states.
That way you only remember 50 things — remembering 100
things and knowing what went with would be too hard.

That's how Thames is smart: he figures out how to do things.

He knows how to open cans and not cut his hands.

Sometimes, when we have crackers, we're careful opening the
long white wrappers so the crackers don't crumble. There are
always one or two broken but we try not to ruin more. Thames
will spread the peanut butter but not too much. That might break
the cracker too. Before he puts the knife back on the counter he
licks the blade to get what food he can and then wipes it with the
bathroom towel.

"Old food makes germs," he always tells me. "We learned that in
school."

We don't eat as often as we do at school and I think Thames
knows why. There's lots of things Thames knows.

At school the adults talk and they tell us what to do. Not just where to sit but how to sit. At home, while Mom does tell us to be still sit or quiet she never tells us how. Thames tells me how. He'll lean over, "do this," and I will. Sometimes, when we're not supposed to talk, Thames will look at me and show my with his eyes and hands.

Sometimes, though, it's not right. Mom still gets angry. Still throws something. Still says words I'm not supposed to say. Thames knows lots of things about what to do when Mom isn't around and knows to be careful when she is. "Shhhhh....quiet.... listen," he whispers when Mom is home. We don't really listen to her - we just don't make any noise. We try not to say anything so she doesn't wake. I don't like what Mom says when she does. Mom once said we didn't need a tv anymore. We still have the tv set though - it just don't light up anymore.

That's why Thames makes the shadows. He got a book from the library, at his school, that shows how to put one hand in front of the next and if you lift certain fingers a certain way the shadow looks like things: a bear, a goat, a face; those are the ones Thames memorized.
Thames is smart that way.

Mom says if the school knew what we have, what we don't, we wouldn't be together. Mom says they would take us away from her and then each other.

"They don't keep brothers and sisters together, ya know." I think Mom knows it's not her we're afraid to be away from.

Thames is standing there. His hands arched in a funny way, two fingers stretching, "can you see the bear?"

It looks more like a rabbit. I'm not as smart as Thames and I've never seen a real bear — but it

looks like a bunny. I want to tell him that but Thames is smiling at me and no one except Thames smiles at me, "Yes, yes I can" and wait to see the goat next.

The Body

Diane struggled for words.
"No, we were away. I thought it was a dead mouse or anything else. I didn't think it was her."
The police officer transcribed her speech. The police officer stood as the other officer, the one with a mustache, stood in the spare bedroom waiting for the medical examiner investigator.

           *   *   *

The body hung.
The body hung from the room's ceiling fan.

           *   *   *

Diane continued.
"A year ago we placed an ad in the newspaper seeking a roommate. Money was tight."
The first officer nodded.

"No phone calls. No mail. She paid rent in cash. I'm not aware of where the money came from."

           *   *   *

The body hung.
The other officer, the one with the mustache, stood waiting.

He looked at the books on the shelves.

           *   *   *

"She stayed in her room during the day and at night she would go out for a walk between the hours of six to ten."
The first officer nodded again.
"She washed every dish immediately after using it, as if she didn't want to leave any evidence, any residue ' ...everything had its place' she said often."
"She said very little though," Diane admitted.

　　　　*　　　　　　　　*　　　　　　　　*

The body hung.
The other officer, the one with a mustache, was tired of looking
at the books and returned his gaze to the body, centered, in the
room.
He looked at his watch. Ten minutes since the call. "It shouldn't be
long," the officer with the mustache thought.

　　　*　　　　　　　　*　　　　　　　　*

"She was a writer. I don't know if she was published." Diane was
beginning to mutter.
"All day, every day, the typewriter could be heard. She started at
8:30 and ended around four. She was writing a novel she told me.
A novel on how a ship is built, or built around a ship's structure...
I forget. The typewriter could be heard every day between 8:30 to
four."
There was an awkward pause.
"Who would want to read a novel about building a ship?"

　　　　　*　　　　　　　*　　　　　　　*

The body hung.
The other officer, the one with a mustache, out of boredom,
grabbed a pencil and poked the body. The tissue was soft.
"More than 24 hours," he thought.

　　　　　*　　　　　　　*　　　　　　　*

"She rarely left her room. Every day, at noon and 2:30 she went
to the bathroom. She had a schedule. At one point, as a joke
to myself really, to see what would happen, I would be in the
bathroom during those times. She just returned to her room and
typed until the next break." Diane was now remembering how
odd she thought of her roommate.
"I always expected her to knock or do something or wait in the
hall. She never did."

*   *   *

The body hung.
The other officer, the one with a mustache, looked at the light switch.
He imagined turning it on.
Would the body swing? he thought to himself.

        *   *   *

"She was always in her room typing."

        *   *   *

The body hung.
The noose was still around the neck.
The medical examiner arrived.
The flash bulbs of the camera's flash illuminated the room.
A blanket was brought in.
Both officers held the body, wrapped, as the investigator cut the rope.

        *   *   *

Diane stood in the kitchen.

        *   *   *

The officers, unaware of how heavy the body was, dropped the body on the floor.
The investigator, on a stepladder, sighed and said, "don't worry, she's already dead" half-joking.
The body now lay on the floor.

        *   *   *

The first officer returned to Diane.
"Is there anyone we can call?" the officer said.
"No one. I don't know of anyone. She never talked about anyone. No friends. No family. She stayed in her room and typed except for her evening walk between six to ten." Diane was now repeating herself.

*   *   *

The body was carried out of the room.
The other officer, the one with a mustache, turned on the light and watched the ceiling fan move.
He imagined the body, the one that had just hung, in full swing circling the room.

*   *   *

"I mean for you," the first officer stated.
"No. I'm fine. Really." She attempted to reassure herself and the officer.

*   *   *

The other officer, the one with a mustache, turned off the light, left the room and shut the door.

*   *   *

The first officer closed his notebook and put his pen back in his front pocket.
"I mean... who would ever read a novel about building a ship?" Diane stuttered.

*   *   *

The room was empty.
All that there was were some books, a typewriter, a bed and reams of blank paper –exactly where one would expect them to be.
Even with the small stain on the floor no one would have guessed that a body hung just moments before.

*   *   *

The officers left.
And Diane stood, in the kitchen, speechless, wondering if the smell, that smell, would ever go away and knowing that tomorrow she would place another ad in the newspaper with a room for rent.

Jayme Juliano

Fireflies

Mom calls me at dinnertime.
Your brother is missing, she says.
(He's done this before.)
It's ok, I tell her.
He'll be found when he's ready.

Or he won't, I think,
and I stay up all night,
watching the news and trying
not to think of the won't,
until the phone rings in the morning.

In the airport, a little boy
with flames on his tennis shoes
smiles at me, a gap
where his front teeth used to be,
and I forget to breathe.

I'm upgraded to first class.
A random courtesy
computer-generated
by the final digits
on my boarding pass.

I don't tell the flight attendant
how my day is going,
but I drink three complimentary
whiskey-and-cokes
before the plane has left the tarmac.

On a backroad in Wisconsin,
buried in green trees and moss,
a motel. A maid, shoes
wearing a blister on her big toe,
opens a door and finds you.

Under the circumstances,
the mortician says, *an open
casket is inadvisable.* Euphemisms
drip from his lips, and I think
How did that gun taste, Joe?

The priest comes to visit,
his job, to comfort.
He refuses to conduct the service.
Under the circumstances, he says,
I'm sure you understand.

Get the fuck out,
Grandma Betty tells him,
the harsh syllable a new taste
on her devout tongue.
She never attends mass again.

We were eight and nine
the summer you lost your teeth.
We stayed up late
to watch the lightning bugs,
catching them in nets,

their tiny lights
flickering among the sweetgrass.
You fell off the swing set
and knocked your front teeth out.
Dad crawled around with a flashlight,

green stains on the knees
of his blue jeans,
looking for a flash of white,
while you stood crying
for the part of you gone forever.

You learned to whistle
through the hole
your teeth had left behind,
your clear notes rising
like fireflies.

[set relations]

[list of mistakes] [sinning eros] [dislocated ethos] [misaligned
ethics] [foraging in acropolis] [lost on tartarus] [set me on fire]
[bronze my flesh] [olive oil and lemon] [crucify me in my hood]
[ssris and a hospital bill] [outstretched youth] [treasure maps
on my thighs] [dont touch me] [dont touch me] [dont touch me]
[dont touch me] [dont touch me] [dont touch me] [dont touch me]
[touch me] [tell me you love me] [your tongue in my ear] [your
hands on my thigh] [aging] [prophetic basements] [glyphs of
pink and gush] [portal in graffiti and piss] [tear my molars out]
[wear them on your neck] [bite my neck] [tie me up] [touch me]
[im yours] [im no one] [gods of love and fire] [pray to hermes]
[run to genet] [hotel hallways] [vacant rooms] [no one is home]
[sliced peaches] [crushed up fruit] [lost good ones to fentanyl]
[clean] [mostly] [sickness] [everything is water] [movement]
[rushing] [fuck me] [fuck you] [thanatos at the carnival][museum
machine] [theft] [gold] [become new] [what is new] [error] [start
over] [insufficient capital] [break your back] [new lords] [death of
myth] [pop culture hedonism] [microplastic orgy] [heated tides]
[drunken trees] [poetics of the anthropocene] [hard to breathe]
[forests on fire] [sunken lips] [logistics] [transportation] [flee
ruined earth] [destroy other planets] [kill] [everything] [pray
to the inverse] [homomorphism] [homoeroticism] [touch me]
[dont perceive me] [kiss my neck] [tell me im pretty] [clasp my
throat] [cover my mouth] [cover my mouth] [bury this body in
the woods] [burn remains] [roll up and smoke] [hot box] [paper
cranes] [on fire] [rewrite] [oral tradition] [story] [elders] [world at
war] [again] [cut] [juxtaposition] [dichotomy] [sameness] [death]
[poetics] [post] [everything] [post] [crime] [murder] [this body]
[fuck me] [fuck you] [room] [closing in] [entropy] [minimized]
[ethical ruin] [utilitarianism] [quantity] [zero] [∅] [emptiness] [no
thing] [cherubim resting in cosmos] [stardust] [break the moon in
two] [one for me] [one for you] [recalibrate] [reset] [everything]
[fuck me] [broken machine] [fluctuations] [the sky is red today]
[breath and ash] [body-machine] [matriarch] [aphrodite] [on fire]

[again] [shovel] [dig up past] [there are no gods left] [nietzsche
on the stake] [out of matches] [uphill] [time travel] [loaded gun]
[load the gun] [armed robbery] [break into--] [the library is
burning] [dostoyevsky torn] [soon to be nothing] [i am soon to be
nothing] [lineage] [ending] [everything is new today] [no interval]
[immediacy] [slow down] [no rush] [smell peaches] [warming]
[the core is turning black] [everything is black] [the scent of
honeysuckle in wind] [kiss the petals] [scatter] there are no more
rules] [everything ends] [we killed the king] [every last one]
[hands together] [unlike prayer] [you are gold] [today][tomorrow]
[yesterday] [tell me im pretty] [fuck me] [dont] [fuck me]
[dont]

[repeat]   [start]   [again]

Alterations

The new bathing suit
was too tight,
grasped at my chest
with underwire.
Metal meant to cause
a pleasing shape
pushed my breath
into an urgent coil.

I cut the neon fabric
and slid out two
steel half-circles.
They clattered
on the counter
and my chest expanded
and I breathed out
corsets and whale bone,
velvet and lace.

Most days, it's like this:
quietly slipping out
of what doesn't fit.
When I'm called "miss"
on the phone
or a stranger says
I am a "lovely woman,"
I smile, sidestep the words, wink
to the squeamish feeling.

Sometimes it's easier to wear
what's given instead
of explaining why
it doesn't fit.

I wish I could tell you
how big it is beyond
the two poles,
the tightly knit binary.

Inside I am ocean,
silver sagebrush drenched
in rain, wind pushing
through outstretched arms,
smooth white granite
held close by river and mud.

What we wear, nothing
but disguise. Listen long
enough and every single
thing is too tight.

Beth Marquez

Doubt

My sweet-tart, my glimmer-hammer,
my queen of pendulum
swing. You're a bit of a safe

cracker in the sciences, unstill,
head cocked and finger to the chalk
board - such swing

and savvy. You're also the worm
in my heart, the soft rot in the center
of the conversation, the secret

that turns the milk sour (magic
like that). Oh, doubt,
you may not be my first

love, but you are the one
that can take any of the others
in a fight. You're a bright light,

less sun and more 'where were you?'
We take the grandest puzzles apart;
we poke gorgeous holes and sing

the body profitable. We make great
ruins of my own delicate bones,
of my own voice threading

through the heavy air, of yet another
April. Doubt, you've shrunk
in the absence of my attentions.

Perhaps I can ignore you to death.
Perhaps you're just biding your time,
listening for the train whistle, waiting for your twin-

certainty – to arrive.

Lori McGinn

Sorrow

Tingles

Bees hover inside
my skin, buzzing muscle
with wings. Nerve endings hum,
tiny legs crawling in swarms –
pins and needles. They collect
the pain like pollen.

I knead flesh to bone
with nettled fingers. Searching
for stingers inside my marrow.
I can never quite reach the prickles –
and my pores hold in their honey.

The Desert

Pain is a rattlesnake. Changing colors,
shedding its skin, it grows and it shrinks,

blends into the background. It stares
with poison eyes, striping brown and black

diamonds across its back. A warning.
Pain is a warning. It hisses at me

when I put a foot on the gas. It rattles
its tail when I walk more than four miles

in a day. Its fangs bite into me when I overdo
exercise at PT. Snakes like the heat,

so I use ice. Snakes like to coil, so I stretch
flesh out. Snakes like to feed, so I toughen

my skin. My muscle grows like an egg.
Snakes hear hatching. I feel a crack.

Testament

Think of the Zoroastrians. The vulture is their undertaker,
stiff-legged in his black cape of shaggy feathers, head
bared to better excavate the body's caverns and plush portals.

In Madagascar's festival, the Turning of the Bones,
families raise, rewrap long-buried corpses, a celebration
of the ancestors. The Norsemen built black death ships
fitted for the longest voyage. Now, some choose to seed
their shrouds with mushroom spores, a congenial option.

Let mushrooms sprout from my bones, pink, tan, or golden
trumpets, silver ears, brown and white, small and neat
as stones. Let them be gnawed by animals, studied by
mycologists, let foragers select the choicest specimens,
as I give back my essence to the Earth.

Some Real Animals Could Pass as Pranks

When I was a kid, my parents used to drive to South Jersey
every weekend. Sometimes we'd pull over at roadside
carnivals, where we would stare at mermaids in a bottle,
the purported skulls of unicorns, a bedraggled bearded lady,
sitting in a folding chair while rude people and their children
gawked and pointed. That is to say, I understand the impulse
to label the natural unnatural.

1

 I wonder whether roadside tourist traps along the Amazon
feature the anableps, perfectly designed, his eyes divided
into four chambers—two above the river's surface, two
below, so he may prey on flies that venture too close
to the water but still see small prey and predators before
they see him. I've never been there, but I'm betting
no billboards clutter those narrow roads. I only know
about this creature from the fact they're popular
with tropical fish hobbyists. They love the beasts
that remind them how weird the world can be.

2

The first time I saw a banana slug, it was in San Francisco's
Muir Woods, among giant redwoods, dim and damp,
shadowed even in full sun. No wonder I couldn't quite
see the bright yellow protoplasm oozing from the bark,
moving fungus. He turned his head to track me, the mobile
eyes on stalks taking in my presence, as I did his.

3

The red-lipped batfish goes knuckling along the sea floor
off the Galapagos. He lives alongside oddities
found nowhere else. Lips red as the wax ones
I used to buy at the local candy store, he's flat,

a flying saucer, propped up on his pectorals,
can barely swim. In this place where iguanas
live mostly underwater, this fish seems to want
to walk on land, a barely functional missing link,
dead end.

Pillow

Ignorance/wills something imagined, which it believes exists.

— Louise Glück

Before I say anything, I must say this:
I returned to the place
where I was tortured—returned
to the woman who tortured me,
the man who watched—
because they weren't people;
they were ideas about people:
Mother. Father. Home.
Even after what happened—
which I tire of talking about,
so much was inactive,
like leaving a lizard too long
to sun in its terrarium
not taking a blowtorch to her,
just forgetting she mattered—
yes, I returned, knowing I was
that reptile and had discussed it
at length with kindly therapists.
But hell's doors are forever
thrown open to thrown-out children,
and, let's not pretend otherwise,
there are some who enjoy hurting
and some who enjoy being hurt.
No they don't.
No agency, no choice, but fault's
a good word, splits below the crust
where disaster begins—
you can see it in the shapes
of spooning continents, rifts so forgotten,

they're scratched themselves on rocks,
and only imagination recaptures what's lost,
which is why I thrilled myself
with longing—like the child
who thinks clouds are pillows
for feathered celestials
who love her, but slowly she learns
clouds are steam, mere water
which, of course, she can drink.

First Nativity

Joseph, at least, wasn't
a speaking part.
                        As if by his silence
acknowledging we have no say
in the divine comedies
we star in.

But I remember
                        the blue mantle
that covered my friend's auburn hair
and her freckles that shimmered
under the stage lights
and the swaddled doll
she held in her lap, and the doll's impossibly long lashes
that fluttered when the eyes opened and closed,
depending on whether you sat the doll
up or laid it down.

                        The cardboard stage set—
sheep donkey cow, the cozy animal warmth
and the quiet knowing that suffused
the scene, that Joseph had chosen
the cleanest hay he could find
and arranged it in the trough just so,
so the golden straws crinkled
as the baby shifted in sleep
in this humblest holiest of hovels,
lit by a cut out (bright yellow)
of a single painted star.

T. R. Poulson

Made From a Rib

God formed a woman's fires in flesh. The power
of figs, of mouth. The flail of words. You read
it all. You drank the wine. Took the bread
from pastors' hands. Blood shed. Body sour
and broken. You were unbroken. The flowers—
again, again—were carried, petals spread
on aisles for other feet. Still, your faith led
you. Still, you abstained. Prayed silent as hours

and years slipped by like song. Pray and wait
no more, forgotten child. Believe the library
of fruit, of serpent. Lure of birds. Let words
open your hair like flesh. Like water. Pleasure
was tendered like a train of sin, of cherry,
before the fall. Eve ate.

Dressage is Like My Love Life

A dressage arena is surrounded by alphabet
letters. Among them, the horse and rider
perfect the walk, the trot, the canter. In
the upper levels they dance.

Lost among letters (so much left unsaid):
the A-K-E-H-C-M-B-F, on cones.
At X, all my horses were beaten, 'til dead,

so to speak. Those circles and canters and lead
changes and halts on the horses I owned
while lost among letters. So much left unsaid:

I dreamt of *passages* and *piaffes* ahead—
all levels of glory, rewards and renown.
Halts, at X. If horses were beaten 'til dead,

I found one: a stallion, high-stepping, well-bred,
his haunches so rippled. I called him my own.
Now lost in old letters, so much left unsaid,

I ask how I fell for him, lured and misled.
His potential held me until I was thrown
(at X) from a horse I then beat until dead.

I show you the ride, not my tears. In the shed,
a man loved me. His touch ached in my bones.
Now lost among letters, not much left unsaid,
my ex lies. I dream he's a horse I beat dead.

Jeremy Ra

Dance Hall at Star Point

On January 21, 2023, a mass shooting occurred in Monterey Park,
California. The shooting happened at Star Ballroom Dance Studio.

We often hoped they were looser—
so they may learn to chassé
and not claim us as the only North star.

Our mothers, who were never the ones
to go to dance halls.

Loose women—
they'd say. They suffer
from being too right all the time.

///

After it happened, I still text you
despite knowing there is little chance
we would personally know any of the star's dusts.

With so many people that came before us,
is there a single square

of land unsmeared by death?

You mention Jack, the boy who first
broke your still-soft heart. I always admired

how you got over him
and tucked your young love away
like a sweater out of season.

///

Not since Jack, have I been to that spot.
Yet something like firecrackers, you recall hearing.

Something like joy fracturing
at the joints.

We joke that our mothers
would never let us off the hook
for wishing they could be more loose—

Be a star—they told us.

Once

I made a home of the dark months—
    like a thrush making safety
        from nothing but lichen and mud.
           Winter was a nest

I built myself, lights on in every room.
    Sometimes I burrow even now.
        Drawn as I am to the scent
           of wet duff, moss like mourning

shawls slung over firs. Sky a poultice
    of gray. This morning I saw a white-tail doe
        cross the road, nostrils steaming, head low,
           her coat the color of stone.

One quick step into the understory
    and she was completely gone.
        It's foolish to think I know
           what she's feeling—the trees

in silent kinship, their needled paths a labyrinth
    for forage and rest. Even the lonely are not
        alone in a forest. Human scent travels far.
           Every animal knows where you are.

Beloved

Bring me your fears. Bring them
like a handful of sad white lilies.
And your sorrow, bring that too,
in the walnut box your father made as a boy.
Corners tightly dovetailed, brass-hinged
heartwood varnished to a sheen, treasures
you left there decades ago still rattling inside.
Dust-colored sparrow wing, a cuff link,
the home address of that boy at summer camp
you couldn't save. Bring me the memory
of your high school sweetheart, the field
behind your house, the long minutes
you breathed for your mother until
the ambulance came. Bring me
your misgivings. Your heartache.
I'll haul it all to the river in a cart strung
with white carnations and won't ask
that you come along. You never did
like to talk about what's gone.
That's okay. I'll come back
with that cart scrubbed clean.

Rachel Rix

In the Fourth Watch We Face: Wind

I thought you were on your way back to me but
those zinnias

you lingered by yesterday must have held

      the fragile spines
                   of dancers in their stems.

Our light scattered well before the war. I see now
there's a line

of broken hulls that will never sink. From the boat deck

    the storm diverges us

               until we rock

any last desire   for each other

               further off the bow.

Untouched—the small of my back, the ridge of your hip, we wonder:
if constellations traced us

what shape we would take.   We adjust

to a new hunger. Waking up earlier we tilt to hear all the tiny
turbines in the universe

      harnessing wisdom,

                              dropping

                                            wombs

into our ears.   Eight times the bell rings

                                            the wind

asking: *what   is   a body?*

Lindsay Rockwell

Brink

All the beautiful parts. Vanish.
Fledglings fall from nest
to earth like feathered weights.
I am falling too.
Because being. Afraid
is what I carry.
As hawk's wingtip kites the stars
the battleship
gray boat of me
rides down river
through summerwood
where light stutters
on doe and fawn
who still in their amaze.
On edge of field.
Listening.
From terror's northern corner—
there's rustling.
As the barrel aims.

Father

1.
there is an elaborate
kind of non-soothing
that is not specific
it is unsteady, unbalanced
as though headlong
we are ravaged

2.
my father's voice protrudes the air
violent— softly ominous

who the hell didn't put my scissors back

3.
he doesn't know I know where he hides his gun
swaddled in a cashmere camel-colored scarf

4.
the night of the tornado he wakes us
flickering four small faces

we follow—oaks thrashing
against each other, hail blisters
alive he marvels,
do you feel how alive?

5.
no matter how hard I concentrate
to untether myself

a sublime ache
begs the fall
yet so admires wings

6.
In a memory
my index & third finger

feel the pulse, faint
then the pulse, gone

7.
fourteen hours later, I walk to my car
spring night wondrous with wetness

a silver spear of lightning
pierces the air, molecules

scatter— rearranging my pupils—
electricity becomes me

8.
sometimes the mind is lightless
that is, there is no light

9.
The night my father dies
owl & bear, raptors
& hyena line up
as he kneels before them

Why was Bukowski the first poet I fell in love with?

I had a father who ground my teeth into salt
Used me to flavor his meal.

Any poet could always bruise me
And make it feel beautiful.
Others could feel like they were doing me the favor
By cutting without drawing blood.

Mean tongued and drunk handed
Fireplace haired
Bottle booted

If I have a crush on you
Don't be flattered.
It's probably an indication
That there is something there
Something subtle below the surface
A claw in the dark
Some carnivore hiding beneath your folds
The shadow you are out running

It's not a compliment, Darling.

I am attracted to the ones who kill.

Angel Rosen

Maybe There Were Other Options

I consult the alternatives. Take my ache prescription.
Load the trunk of the car with my best ideas and ugliest dresses.
Something starts to rattle back there,
but I don't ask its name.
I'll be gone for two weeks or the rest of my life.

It's sad here. Right here. My exact latitude and longitude
is the most depressing.
I am always having the worst time.
I wish there was a cure for loneliness.
I wish I was the cure, because then everyone would love me.
But if everyone loved me, I think I would need to be alone.

Have you done it all? Have you ever stopped in the middle
of sex and thought,
I can't keep doing this because I'm allergic to friction?
Have you found the other lost girls?
They're sitting beside married men,
and they're accepting the men's fancy, then disappearing.
Once they disappear, they're really found.

Have you done nothing? Have you ever stopped mid-sentence
when you're begging someone to stay and thought,
I can't keep doing this because you're allergic to friction?
Dinner will never be ready again.

Have you made serious attempts?
On your life?
At achievement?
Applications, affairs, disorderly conducts?
Have you been arrested or are the marks
on your wrists from a different restraint?

No one says a suicide was someone unbeloved.
The obituary never says *thank god.*

When I die, I just want a list that reads
Thank you to everyone who made life more bearable
(in order of importance at time of death):

Basically, I have never wanted to die less than I do now.
Sometimes I even look out the window and imagine
the world with me in it.

Sometimes, I go into the world.
I'm not a lost girl. I just don't understand direction.
All of my solutions are North. All of the people
I could make less lonely
are currently giving head to someone else.
This doesn't bother me anymore.
Nothing bothers me anymore, a needle in a haystack,
a banjo in a crosswalk, a kite without a sky.

I wake up tomorrow and saw that the car drove away without me.
The gravel thinks I can drive.
I can't report the car lost or stolen, just because it had an idea.
Sometimes I have ideas and then I do them.
In the middle of doing them, I think
maybe there were other options.

Nova Larkin Schrage

Loving Kindness Meditation on the SIXT Rent a Car PA at 4am

YOU ARE TRESPASSING. YOUR PRESENCE IS UNWANTED, AND YET YOU PERSIST. TODAY YOU WOKE UP. TODAY YOU DID NOT SELL YOUR INBREATH. TODAY YOU DID NOT SELL YOUR OUTBREATH. YOU ARE TRESPASSING AND YET YOU WISH TO FEEL AT EASE. YOU ARE TRESPASSING AND YET YOU WISH THAT OTHER TRESPASSERS BE FREE FROM PAIN. PLEASE LEAVE THE AREA. NOTICE: DO YOU FEEL WELCOME HERE? THERE ARE WARMER PLACES FOR YOU TO BE. REJOIN THE AREA CONTAINING THOSE WHO LOVE YOU. THIS AREA IS UNDER VIDEO SURVEILLANCE AND YOU HAVE BEEN RECORDED.

New Disease

<table>
<tr><td>

You always said that
people have sexes"
what it means
to assign me to a gender
to label my emotions
disordered, to allot me
per year, to ask that my name
correct

</td><td>

"words have genders,
and I've been thinking about
to be a prescriptivist:
"for insurance purposes",
subclinical, my behavior
40 hours of sick time
auto-
to yours.

</td></tr>
</table>

//

<table>
<tr><td>

A lover once told me that
grow into easy adults,
into difficult adults"
what it means
how sometimes the form
auditory,
visual) and I
all my cookies.
and let one
from my fingers
as I walk home
to go mad
I've tried
to deserve accommodations
the paperwork. I
I'm on medical leave, because
while asking about my vacation

</td><td>

"difficult children
while easy children grow
and I've been thinking about
to be non-binary:
only has two options (mobility,
thinking/learning,
quit. I erase
I tear up the form
small strip slip
every few blocks
alone. I've tried
as quietly as possible.
to be disabled enough
but abled enough to complete
haven't told you
isn't misgendering me
what's easiest for you?

</td></tr>
</table>

//

<table>
<tr><td>

You always said that
people get angry."
what
means
         to be   a crazy bitch—

to have to teach myself
"help"
reading

</td><td>

"*cows* go mad,
and I've been thinking about
it

a dead cow

how to spell
without a doctor
"hospitalize"

</td></tr>
</table>

Amanda Leigh Smith

51 Miles to the Ocean

"Life on the LA River"

"As Above, So Below"

Malapai Hill in Joshua Tree National Park

Deidre Sullivan

Back of the Tapestry

I turn the tapestry over to see
the carefully wrought knots,
dangling, shaggy threads,
the bumps and nubs
and the smooth sections
where it went well:

all you did, all you tried
to create,
so painstakingly,
such beauty.

You signed your name in chalk
on the back.
I can barely make out the letters but
I read your name,
and say it aloud
to myself
knowing you are there
behind it all,

still stitching,
still knotting.

I love your work, this side
the most.

Teutophobia
Kristallnacht, Nov 9, 1938 – Nov 10, 1938

Entourage of mink coats/ chokers high
hats/ of white wood orange peel/ of pearls
rugs buttons in a cobalt jar/ of gabardine
pale chambray/ of blue blood thin blood—
gemmed vial for both— trinkets tassels shams
and Schubert/ of all will: shrinking and ill
will/ what's seen/unseen: the chiseled
nettles: the exits the life-list the sudden
tunnels/ the blade and socket/ the brew the
breath the barefoot/ the swaddled/ the thin
river that quickly deepened/ the shards of
synagogues/ the synagogues/ the muscle/
of goosestep/ the wet leather of Krystall/ of
Nacht/ of the accused/ and those who
bowed/ the laid on fields of bone/ the stars/
boldened yellowed/ hung from the sky/

Oh/ Mother.

Ben Trigg

A Brief History of Cremation

It begins with a father,
a room full of silence,
and a daughter lying broken on the floor.
In his madness he thinks of the phoenix,
imagines his child as a firebird,
finds solace in the possibility of rebirth.

Entomology Sings a Lullaby

The honey can wait,
tomorrow's pollen, patient and plentiful.
The hill is fully built,
the food stores overflow.
All my little darlings, it is time for the world to grow quiet.
Still your wings and reaching mandibles,
silence the harps of your legs.
Sweet fireflies, let darkness overtake you.
Tonight I watch over you all, predator and prey.
You are all safe in my arms.
This is my gift - a moment's rest
before you busy the waking world.

Lizzie Wann

Luck

it starts with a sparrow
I check on the small bird that claims
narrow underside ledge of an awning
outside my dining room window
I don't expect it to stay, but every night
it remains perched there, still & silent

there are also crickets in the kitchen
it's said you shouldn't kill a cricket, but some have
met their fate on linoleum or in the sink
yet there are always others the next day, chirping

when I talk to my sister, we knock on wood
whenever we don't want to jinx whatever we said
she crosses herself every time she leaves the house

I returned from Greece with my own evil eye mati,
travel with a weeping Buddha small enough to
hold while the plane takes off into the firmament

who hasn't picked up a penny or crossed their fingers?

maybe someday I'll have a red door
paint my porch in haint blue
get a horseshoe tattoo
but for now, my luck might simply be
taking my aging mother
to the library in February

Aruni Wijesinghe

We regret to inform you we won't be publishing

your white lemon blossoms –
though your rendering of the petals
made our assistant editor sigh
and remember his first wife, the one

who always wore a summer dress,
even in early February. The shirred voile
drifting around her shapely calves,
the puffed sleeves tucked inside a down jacket.

We so appreciate you taking the time
to describe the scent of earth clinging
to your fingertips; please understand
that this note in no way reflects

the way we feel about the coming Spring.

Love Poem

He rolled home from the funeral sweaty and sad.

Before the illness, the punishments were less discrete.

My favorite gift was the boot glass, its cold shiver.

Behind him one-hundred church books fell.

The dog was at the front door, panting like rattle grass.

They asked us all to please remember conditioner and a belt.

There was a jawbone to mark the bad spot.

Last year twenty-nine people ate a single shark.

The socks were stained with soil.

The airplane refused legs, trousers, even kisses.

He didn't believe the warnings and died among fishmongers and tiger moths.

Situations scared him most of all.

Then, paper was scarce and everyone's faces hurt.

They found our bodies beneath ten-thousand years of feathers.

Anne Yarbrough

Wing Postmortem
Mary, after The Annunciation

Once I'd killed the angel
I found the part
that charmed me most
was his wing.
How it had been made.

I laid its feathers
on the ground
in rows ordered by size.
Walked around them.
Memorized.
Rearranged them by color
and after that
according to the sound
each one made
as it descended.

Some days
I thought it had been
nothing but a trick,
like the swirl
of the magician's cape
as he's sawing a woman
in half. How, first,
you're taken by surprise,
then how you think,
There must be more to it.

I threaded my needle
with wet strings of blood
and sewed the feathers
back together, badly.
Hung the whole thing,
dripping, on my wall,
passed it off as folk art.

I stood in the doorway
and breathed it in,
searching
its elusive mechanism.

I Am August

My strawberries sweet,
my tomatoes heavy
on the vine.
And when
a June brushes past,
wading through the dappled sunlight
of sidewalk beneath sycamore tree
his cherries are enough
to make me grieve.

Transference

Take the scarf with you, he says.

> In order to extract their scent,
> petals or whole flowers are placed
> on a large framed plate of glass,
> called chassis,
> smeared with a layer of animal fat.

He unties the scarf from his neck,
gives it to me.

> The scent is allowed to diffuse
> into the fat over the course of 1-3 days.
> The process is then repeated by replacing
> the spent botanicals with fresh ones
> until the fat has reached a desired degree of
> fragrance saturation.

Thank you, I say.
We are at the Heathrow airport.
My plane leaves in twenty minutes.

> This procedure was developed
> in the 18th century
> for the production of high-grade concentrates.
> It is called enfleurage.

The scarf is the color of wine,
with small polka dots,
slightly frayed,
warm like a sleeping dog.

Tamara Zbrizher

In line at the Wawa

I.

The man behind me inches closer
says something about my leopard print shoes
something about them is *wild*
meaning something inside me is *wild*
hoping the *something wild* inside me
will take him for *wild* ride
meaning, let him on

II.

The wild something inside me
is riddening
The pill bucks
I grip the counter
pay & smile
the smile
the *no-but-thanks* smile
the *nevermind-the-death-ripening-inside-me* smile
the *can't-you-see-the-death-ripening-inside-me?* smile
the *broken-horse* smile

a woman's smile (a smile that every woman carries in her purse)

The smile that always works
And it works. Always. *Wild!*

III.

He yells, "baby wait!"

No baby

I'm out the door
hobbling home
first of the blood
dripping down my leg
all the way
down Central
and I don't wipe it
I don't dare

About the Contributors

Dr. Jennifer L. Abod Her poems appear in *Artemis Journal, Sinister Wisdom, One Art Journal, The Metro Washington Weekly, Wild Crone Wisdom,* and *Silver Birch Press.* She is an award-winning documentary filmmaker and radio broadcaster, a former media specialist, and Assistant Professor of Communications and Women's Studies. www.jenniferabod.com

Dania Ayah Alkhouli is a Syrian Pushcart Prize nominated writer, poet, editor, and author of three poetry & prose collections. Her work centers on survivorship, feminism, domestic violence/sexual assault, death & grief, religion & culture, and her homeland, Syria. Alkhouli is currently pursuing her M.B.A. while working in real estate investments management, as well as serving as the creative director and co-founder at A COUNTRY CALLED SYRIA, a nonprofit traveling arts-based exhibition showcasing Syria's history and culture.

Robin Axworthy is a retired teacher and working writer who lives in Southern California. Her work has been published in various anthologies, including: *Is it Hot in Here or Is It Just Me?* (Beautiful Cadaver Project), *Cathexis Northwest Press,* June-Aug 2019 (Cathexis Northwest Press), and *Dark Ink: An Anthology Inspired by Horror* and *Shit Men Say to Me* (Moon Tide Press.) Her chapbook, *Crabgrass World* was published in March 2020 and is available from Moon Tide Press as well. She has won various awards for her work, including the jojo show contest (June 2022). She leads the poetry workshop for the Writer's Club of Whittier and is active in the local poetry community.

Kay E. Bancroft (they/them) is a queer non-binary writer, poet, editor, educator, and artist based in Cincinnati, OH. They hold an MFA in Poetry from Randolph College, and a BA from the University of Cincinnati. You can find their writing in *Passengers Journal, Honey Literary, GASHER, Voicemail Poems, Hooligan Magazine, The Rumpus,* & more. Explore more at www.kayebancroftpoet.com

Lyra Bateman is a poet and mixed-media artist. Her experiences as a disabled woman living with Dissociative Identity Disorder and Post-traumatic Stress Disorder shape her work. Her creative process is defined by collaborating with her alters, who work together using a range of materials and perspectives to create a single piece. By telling her story through her work, she shares her unique voice.

Mary Beth Becker was raised in the woods north of Omaha, Nebraska, but lives with her wife in Saint Paul, Minnesota. Her poems have been published in *Mud Season Review, Split Rock Review, Hobart,* and *West Trade Review.* She is a Pushcart Prize and Best-of-the-Net nominee, and a friend to all rivers.

Erik Brockbank is a writer living in Santa Cruz and working as a postdoctoral researcher at Stanford University. This is his first poetry publication.

Paola Bruni is the author of the epistolary *How Do You Spell the Sound of Crickets* (Paper Angel Press), a two-time Pushcart Prize nominee and winner of various poetry awards including the Muriel Craft Bailey Poetry Prize. Her poems have appeared in *The Southern Review, Ploughshares, The Birmingham Review, SWWIM,* and *Comstock Review,* among others. She resides in Aptos, California.

Alexandra Burack is a Pushcart Prize-nominated poet, author of *On the Verge* (Plinth Books), editor, and Poetry Reader for *The Los Angeles Review.* Her recent work appeared in *The Sewanee Review, The Blue Mountain Review, Ink & Marrow, FreezeRay Poetry, $ Poetry is Currency,* and *Poetica Magazine,* and is forthcoming in *Broad River Review* and *Orlando.* She is the Founding Editor of *Lumina* and *Invert,* and the recipient of poetry grants from the CT Commission on the Arts, the Ludwig Vogelstein Foundation, and the Haymarket Foundation. She teaches currently as Adjunct Professor of Creative Writing at Chandler-Gilbert Community College (AZ).

Jessica June Cato (she/they) is a writer, poet, and Lead Astrologer at The Poetry Lab. Her work has been published by *Nightingale & Sparrow, Sampaguita Press, Chicanx Writers and Artists Association,* and *Querencia Press*. Her debut poetry chapbook, *Through The Red Door's Open Maw,* is available now from Beyond The Veil Press. Her favorite things include making memes, Nintendo switch, and her two small poodles. You can find her on socials talking about Astrology For Poets, her series of articles, videos, podcast episodes and writing workshops on astrology, poetry, and the ways they intertwine @jessjunewrites

Sarah ChristianScher teaches biology by day, by night she can be found searching for inspiration at the bottom of a can of La Croix. She has been featured in *Like a Girl: Perspectives on Feminine Identity, Dark Ink: A Poetry Anthology Inspired by Horror, Short Poems Ain't Got Nobody to Love,* and *Voice-mail Poetry*. Sarah can often be found lurking at the Two Idiots Peddling Poetry reading in Orange, CA.

Alexis Rhone Fancher is published in *Best American Poetry, Rattle,Verse Daily, The American Journal of Poetry, Plume, Diode,* and elsewhere. She's authored ten poetry collections, most recently EROTIC: New & Selected (NYQ Books), and *DUETS (Small Harbor Press)* an ekphrastic chapbook written with Virginia poet, Cynthia Atkins. *BRAZEN* , an erotic, full-length collection, the follow up to *EROTIC,* published in 2023, again from NYQ. A coffee table book of Alexis' photographs of Southern California poets will be published by Moon Tide Press in 2024. She lives in the Mojave Desert with her husband, Fancher. They have an incredible view. www.alexisrhonefancher.com

Lauren Frost (she/her) is a journalist, comedian, and writer from Chicago. These are her first published works of poetry.

Newark, NJ native **Ysabel Y. González,** received her BA from Rutgers University and an MFA in Poetry from Drew University. Ysabel has received invitations to attend VONA, Tin House, CantoMundo and BOAAT Press workshops. In her work, Ysabel explores her neurodivergence, Borinquen roots, and how to engage with tenderness in a complicated world. She is a Pushcart Prize nominee and the author of *Wild Invocations* (Get Fresh Books, 2019). You can find her in New Jersey living with her husband and two furbabies, crafting, tending to her garden, and reading tarot. Visit www.ysabelgonzalez.com for more.

AE Hines is the author of *Adam in the Garden* (Charlotte Lit Press, 2024) and *Any Dumb Animal* (Main Street Rag, 2021). His poems have been widely published in such journals as *The Southern Review, Prairie Schooner, Rattle, The Sun,* and *Alaska Quarterly.* He received his MFA from Pacific University and divides his time between Charlotte, North Carolina and Medellín, Colombia. www.aehines.net

Ciarán Hodgers is an Irish, multi-award winning spoken word poet. His second poetry collection, *Solastalgia,* was published by Burning Eye Books in November 2023 and explores the intersection of mental health and climate change, spirituality and colonialism. He has been nominated for the Pushcart Prize 2020 and won the Sean Dunne National Young Writer 2010, an International Pangaea Poetry Slam Champion 2015 and the Word War 3 Slam Champion. www.ciaranhodgers.sumupstore.com/

LeAnne Hunt (she/her) has a master's in English and taught at Parkland College and Austin Community College. She has worked as a freelance writer and proofreader, tutor, library assistant and data reviewer for an environmental lab. She misses her lab coat and the clink of test tubes. She has poems published in *Cultural Weekly, Spillway, Honey & Lime,* and *Lullaby of Teeth: An Anthology of Southern California Poets.* She publishes a blog of writing prompts and apologies at www.leannehunt.com.

Alexis Jaimes is the proud son of Mexican immigrants and resides in Santa Ana, CA, his home. He believes in aliens and words. Previously published in *Raspa Magazine, Polemical Zine, Alegria Magazine*, and featured at the award-winning Fullerton Museum Center in an exhibit titled "Fullerton Art Town: What Feels like Home" in 2023. He earned his BA in English from California State University, Long Beach, and an MS and teaching credential from California State University, Fullerton to become a bilingual elementary teacher. He aims to empower and uplift his community through words.

Amy E. Boyle "bonk" Johnston, from Santa Cruz, California, is an artist and writer based in Rochester, NY. She holds an MFA from Visual Studies Workshop. She has been published in *The Philadelphia Inquirer, LA Weekly* and *The New York Times*. She is a former resident artist at the Flower City Arts Center and is on the board of the Rod Serling Memorial Foundation.

Jayme Juliano is a pianist and poet from Orange County, California, where she has been a performer and teacher for the past ten years. When she's not reading or playing the piano, she enjoys needlework, gardening, and going to theme parks. Jayme holds a degree in English literature from California State University, Long Beach, and lives with her teenage son and two black cats.

Eros Livieratos (He/They) is a Greek-Belizean writer & artist whose work focuses on the intersection of identity, aesthetics, and capital in the Anthropocene. Eros has published poetry, fiction, non-fiction, comics, photography, and film score work. They can usually be found making harsh noise & screaming in your local basement.

Emilie Lygren is a nonbinary poet and outdoor educator whose work emerges from the intersections between scientific observation and poetic wonder. Her first book of poetry, *What We Were Born For,* was chosen by the Young People's Poet Laureate as the February 2022 Book Pick for the Poetry Foundation. She lives in California, where she wonders about oaks and teaches poetry in local classrooms. Find more of her work and words on Instagram (@emlygren) and on her website www.emilielygren.com

Beth Marquez has been published in Moon Tide Press, Valley of the Contemporary Poets, and Ugly Mug anthologies. Her poems were selected for *Damfino literary journal*'s debut issue and the *Like a Girl* anthology from Lucid Moose Press, which nominated her poem Shedding for a Pushcart Prize. She is a 2017 Pink Door Fellow. She holds three mathematics degrees, has been writing and performing poetry for over half her life, and was once stranded on a deserted island.

Lori McGinn has baked 1,000's of cookies and written some poems. She likes to bake, loves to watch as the sun sets over the ocean. She loves her family, her Moon, her Jesus. She has been published in *Spillway, Laguna Poets* series, and *Tebot Bach*. She lives in Whittier with her husband Daniel McGinn.

Makena Metz is an LA native who writes for the page, screen, and stage. She has a MFA in Creative Writing and MA in English from Chapman University's dual degree program. Makena is a proud member of DGA, ASCAP, WIA, and the SCL. Find her work on *Coverfly, NPX*, and follow her @makenametz on Tiktok, IG, FB, Twitter, and check out www.makenametz.com

Robbi Nester is the author of 4 books of poetry and editor of three anthologies. A retired college educator, she hosts and curates two poetry series on Zoom. Learn more about her work at her website, www.robbinester.net.

Dion O'Reilly's collection, *Ghost Dogs* (Terrapin Books 2020) was runner-up for The Catamaran Prize and shortlisted for several awards, including The Eric Hoffer Award. Her second book *Sadness of the Apex Predator* was published by University of Wisconsin's Cornerstone Press in 2024. Her work appears in *The Sun, New Ohio Review, Cincinnati Review, Rattle, Narrative, The Slowdown*, and elsewhere. She facilitates private workshops, hosts a podcast at *The Hive Poetry Collective,* and is a reader for *Catamaran Literary Quarterly*. She splits her time between a ranch in the Santa Cruz Mountains and a residence in Bellingham, Washington.

Derek N. Otsuji was born on Oahu and is the author of *The Kitchen of Small Hours* (SIU Press, 2021), selected by Brian Turner for the Crab Orchard Poetry Series and featured in *Honolulu Magazine's* "Essential Hawaii Books You Should Read." He is a 2019 Tennessee Williams Scholar and a 2023 Longleaf Fellow in Poetry. Recent work has appeared in *32 Poems, Southern Review,* and *The Threepenny Review.*

T. R. Poulson, a University of Nevada alum and proud Wolf Pack fan, lives in San Mateo, California. Her work has appeared, or is forthcoming, in various journals, including *Best New Poets, Gulf Coast,* and *Booth.* She supports her writing habit by delivering for UPS in Woodside, California. Find her at www.trpoulson.com, and on social media as @trpoulson.

Jeremy Ra is a queer, Chinese-Korean-American poet living in Los Angeles. A Pushcart and Best-of-the-Net nominee, he was the recipient of the 2022 Morton Marcus Poetry Prize and a finalist for the Steve Kowit Poetry Prize. His poems have appeared in *I-70 Review, Cultural Daily, San Diego Poetry Annual,* and *Catamaran Literary Reader,* among others. He is a co-host of the video series, Poetry.la. His first chapbook, *Another Way of Loving Death,* has been published by Moon Tide Press.

Emily Ransdell divides her time between Camas, Washington and Manzanita, Oregon, where she teaches poetry through the Hoffman Center for the Arts. Her work has appeared in *Tar River Poetry, New Letters, Rattle, Poetry Northwest,* and elsewhere. Her first collection, *One Finch Singing,* won the 2022 Lewis Award from Concrete Wolf Press and was published in 2023.

Rachel Rix has published and has forthcoming work in *Wrath-Bearing Tree, War Literature & the Arts, The Tiger Moth Review, Verdad, Right Hand Pointing,* the anthology *When There Are Nine* (as well as being shortlisted for the Fish Anthology 2020 poetry contest in Ireland). Rix earned an MFA from the University of Nevada, Reno at Lake Tahoe, and she works as a CMT in Sacramento--where she lives with her husband, Adam, and their two cats, Floppy and Leo.

Lindsay Rockwell is poet-in-residence for the Episcopal Church of Connecticut. She's recently published, or forthcoming in *Humana Obscura, Poetry Northwest, Poet Lore, Radar, Spillway, SWIMM* every day, among others. Her collection, *GHOST FIRES,* was published by Main Street Rag, April 2023. She's received fellowships from Vermont Studio Center and Edith Wharton/The Mount residency. Lindsay is also an oncologist.

Melissa Rose is a professional spoken word poet, playwright and mental health practitioner. In over 20 years of performing and writing she has been a team member of 5 National Poetry Slam Teams, was a featured performer at over 30 venues in Germany and Austria, and has been published in both print and online publications. Her solo poetry monologue, "Baggage" has been featured in numerous New York theater festivals including The United Solo Festival and the Downtown Urban Arts Festival, where it received the award for Best Play. She is currently pursuing a PhD in Expressive Therapies.

Angel Rosen is a lesbian poet living near Pittsburgh. She can be found reading Plath, sharing anecdotes, and collaborating with artists within the Amanda Palmer community. She is passionate about mental health and friendship. Find her at www.angelrosen.com or on social media at @Axiopoeticus.

Nova Larkin Schrage is a mad disabled poet. Co enjoys cats, being a legal adult, singing, thinking critically about the world, loving, and being loved. Co would like to extend cos well wishes to trespassers everywhere, perhaps especially The Citizens' Commission to Investigate the FBI (based simply on their Wikipedia page). One could read more about Nova and cos work at www.nova.repair.

Amanda Leigh Smith makes nature-focused digital paintings, photography, and paper cuts that encourage people to consider the urban-wildland interface of Southern California and its biodiversity. In 2021, she became a Certified California Naturalist and created www.losangelesisnotadesert.com, where her writing and art challenges stereotypes about nature within cities. Her work is inspired by LA's unique seasons and her animal and plant neighbors. Amanda's art has been featured at the Jacksonville Dance Theater's *In Here/ Out There: A Digital Dance Series*, the LA River X Pop-Up Gallery, and America's Great Outdoors at the LA County Fair.

Deidre Sullivan is writer who also works in the field of cultural strategy and insights, often with a focus on semiotics. She divides her time between New York City and the Hudson Valley.

Carine Topal's work has appeared in *The Best of the Prose Poem, Greensboro Review, Iron Horse Literary Review*, and many other journals and anthologies. *Bed of Want*, her 2nd collection, won the 2007 Robert G. Cohen Prose Poetry Award. She is the recipient of the 2015 Briar Cliff Review Award for Poetry. Her prize-winning book, *Tattooed*, won the Palettes and Quills Chapbook contest. Topal's 5th collection, *In Order of Disappearance*, was published in 2018 by Pacific Coast Poetry Series. She teaches poetry and memoir workshops in Southern California.

Ben Trigg dreams of being Truly Outrageous, striving to be a safe space for all, but especially the queer community. He is one third of Two Idiots Peddling Poetry at the Ugly Mug in Orange, California, a weekly series that has been running since 2000. Ben's poetry has been described (by him) as the sweet spot junction of heartfelt, pop culture, and comedy. His collection *Kindness from a Dark God* came out on Moon Tide Press in 2007. He co-edited the anthology *Don't Blame the Ugly Mug: 10 Years of 2 Idiots Peddling Poetry*. When all else fails, Ben goes to Disneyland.

Lizzie Wann is a long-time poet who helped develop slams, readings, and other happenings in the San Diego scene once upon a time. Her first poetry collection, *The Hospice Bubble & Other Devastating Affirmations*, was published by Puna Press (San Diego) in 2019.

Aruni Wijesinghe is a project manager, ESL teacher, erstwhile bellydance instructor and occasional sous chef. A Pushcart Prize and Best of the Net nominee, she has been published nationally and internationally online and in print journals and anthologies. She is the author of three poetry collections: *2 Revere Place* a love letter to her family and miraculous childhood in New York; *The Litany of Missing*, a meditation on loss, longing and love; and *Bedside Manners*, a rumination on the American healthcare system. You can follow her on social media at @aruniwrites (Instagram and Twitter) or on her website at www.aruniwrites.com

Adele Elise Williams is the author of *Wager* selected by Patricia Smith for the 2024 Miller Williams Poetry Series. She is a PhD candidate in Literature and Creative Writing at The University of Houston where she serves as Nonfiction Editor for Gulf Coast. With Dana Levin, Adele co-edited the most recent volume of the Unsung Masters Series on poet Bert Meyers. Her work can be found in *Poetry Northwest, The Georgia Review, Crazyhorse, Guernica, Cream City Review, The Florida Review, Beloit Poetry Journal*, and elsewhere.

Anne Yarbrough's first collection, *Refinery* (Broadkill River Press), received the 2021 Dogfish Head Poetry Prize. Her poems have appeared in *Poet Lore, Gargoyle, CALYX Journal, Cider Press Review, SWWIM Every Day, THRUSH* Poetry Journal and elsewhere. Her poem, "Smoke," was a finalist in *The 2023 Best Spiritual Literature Awards in Fiction, Nonfiction, and Poetry* (Orison Press, forthcoming). She's a 2023 Delaware Division of the Arts Fellow. She lives along the lower Delaware River, which was once called Lenapewihittuck.

Aubrey Yarbrough studies poetry at The MFA Program for Writers at Warren Wilson. Her poems have appeared in *New American Writing* and *The Los Angeles Press*. She lives in Los Angeles.

Mariano Zaro is the author of six books of poetry, most recently *Decoding Sparrows* (What Books Press, Los Angeles) and *Padre Tierra* (Olifante, Zaragoza, Spain). His poems and short stories have been published in anthologies and literary journals in Spain, Mexico and the United States. His translations include *Buda en llamas* by Tony Barnstone and *Cómo escribir una canción de amor* by Sholeh Wolpé. He is a professor of Spanish at Rio Hondo Community College (Whittier, California). www.marianozaro.com

Tamara Zbrizher is a Ukrainian American poet. Her work has been published in various journals and anthologies and has been nominated for a Pushcart Prize and Best of The Net. She is the recipient of the 2021 NJ Poets Prize. Her first full-length collection *Tell Me Something Good* was released from Get Fresh Books in 2019. She is the co-founder of Yes&:NJ Creates, an organization that offers free resources to NJ writers, and a founding member of the feminist poetry collective, Write On!Poetry Babes. She lives in the woods of New Jersey.

About the Editors

torrin a. greathouse is a transgender cripple-punk poet and essayist. She has received fellowships from the National Endowment for the Arts, the Ragdale Foundation, and the University of Arizona Poetry Center. Their work is published in POETRY, Ploughshares, and The Kenyon Review. She is the author of *Wound from the Mouth of a Wound* (Milkweed Editions, 2020) winner of the Kate Tufts Discovery Award, and DEED (Wesleyan University Press, 2024). She teaches at the Rainier Writing Workshop, the low-residency MFA program at Pacific Lutheran University.

Rachel McKibbens is a poet, playwright, organizer and two-time New York Foundation for the Arts poetry fellow. She is the author of three critically acclaimed books of poetry, *blud* (Copper Canyon, 2017) *Pink Elephant* (Small Doggies, 2009) and *Into the Dark & Emptying Field* (Small Doggies, 2012) a finalist for the Paterson Poetry Prize. Her chapbook, MAMMOTH, was the 1st runner up for the David Blair Poetry Prize. McKibbens has appeared on two seasons of Russell Simmons presents Def Poetry Jam on HBO, was the 2001 West Coast Regional Poetry Slam Champion and the 2011 National Underground Individual Poetry slam champion. For four years McKibbens taught poetry through the Healing Arts Program at Bellevue Hospital and continues to teach creative writing and lecture across the country as an advocate for mental health awareness and victims of violence and sexual abuse. In 2012, McKibbons founded The Pink Door Writing Retreat, an annual retreat held exclusively for non-men writers of color. In 2022, McKibbons was the subject of the podcast *We Were Three*, from The New York Times and the producers of Serial. She currently lives in upstate New York.

Ellen Webre is a biracial, Taiwanese-American poet, born in Hong Kong and raised in California. She is a social media marketing specialist, editor, and videographer for Moon Tide Press, is a co-host of Two Idiots Peddling Poetry, a member of the Tesoro Collective, a staff member of The Definitive Soapbox open mic and is the new managing editor of *Spillway Magazine*. Ellen's debut book, *A Burning Lake of Paper Suns* (Moon Tide Press 2021), won a Best Indie Author Award for poetry cover design. Her poem "Metaphors for My Body in Midwinter" has been nominated for the Pushcart Prize 2021. Ellen's other poems have most recently been published in *A Moon of One's Own, FreezeRay, Sh!t Men Say to Me: Anthology in Response to Toxic Masculinity, Dark Ink: A Poetry Anthology Inspired by Horror,* and *Voicemail Poems.*

Shelly Holder is a participant of the 2023-2024 Lighthouse Writer's Poetry Collective, where she is working on her first manuscript, *Naming the Marrow.* She facilitates various poetry events online, including workshops and book clubs, and serves as the chapter lead for the San Gabriel Valley branch of Women Who Submit, a non-profit organization seeking to promote the publication of women and women identifying writers, especially in top tier literary journals. In her non-poetry life, she is pursuing a certificate in Library Sciences, while trying keep her houseplants alive and her puppy calm(ish). Her work can be found at various publications including *Iron Horse Review* and *Ponder Review,* among others, which are listed in full at her website www.shellyholder.com.

Acknowledgements

"No Small Happiness" by AE Hines first appeared in his second collection, *Adam in the Garden*, published by Charlotte Lit Press.

"Dirgelings" and "Clearing" have been previously published in *Solastalgia* (Burning Eye Books, 2023)

"The Desert" and "Tingles" by Makena Metz originally appeared in *The Literary Hatchet #36, 2023*.

"Beloved" by Emily Ransdell first appeared in Kestrel, under the title "Husband, bring me." "Once" appears in her collection *One Finch Singing*, published by Concrete Wolf Press.

"New Disease" by Nova Larkin Schrage was previously published in [Open Minds Quarterly].

"Brink" by Lindsay Rockwell has been published by *CARVE*, Winter 2024, under a different title, "Dear Unknown."

Submit to *Spillway Magazine: Volume 3, Issue 1*

Thank you for reading *Spillway Magazine: Volume 2, Issue 30*—the final issue of Volume 2. We look forward to beginning a brand-new chapter with *Spillway Magazine* with the start of the next volume, and we hope you consider submitting to it.

Our guest editors will be **Steven Reigns** (inaugural Poet Laurate of West Hollywood and author of *A Quilt for David*) and **Douglas Manuel** (a Borchard Foundation Center on Literary Arts Fellow and author of *Trouble Funk*). We are very excited to have them on board to guest edit the first issue of Volume 3.

Volume 3, Issue 1 will be a themed issue: we are looking for work (poetry, prose, flash fiction, short story, and/or black and white visual art that speaks to the subject matter of reinvention, rebirth, renewal, reincarnation, revival, recycle, etc.

Submissions will open July 1st, 2024, and will run through September 30th, 2024, through Submittable. For guidelines and instructions to submit please visit www.moontidepress.com/spillway or follow us on Facebook and Instagram @moontidepress.

We look forward to the future and reading your work!

Eric Morago
Moon Tide Press
Publisher

Also Available from Moon Tide Press

At the Table of the Unknown, Alexandra Umlas (2019)
The Book of Rabbits, Vince Trimboli (2019)
Everything I Write Is a Love Song to the World,
    David McIntire (2019)
Letters to the Leader, HanaLena Fennel (2019)
Darwin's Garden, Lee Rossi (2019)
Dark Ink: A Poetry Anthology Inspired by Horror (2018)
Drop and Dazzle, Peggy Dobreer (2018)
Junkie Wife, Alexis Rhone Fancher (2018)
The Moon, My Lover, My Mother, & the Dog,
    Daniel McGinn (2018)
*Lullaby of Teeth: An Anthology of Southern
    California Poetry* (2017)
Angels in Seven, Michael Miller (2016)
A Likely Story, Robbi Nester (2014)
Embers on the Stairs, Ruth Bavetta (2014)
The Green of Sunset, John Brantingham (2013)
The Savagery of Bone, Timothy Matthew Perez (2013)
The Silence of Doorways, Sharon Venezio (2013)
Cosmos: An Anthology of Southern California Poetry (2012)
Straws and Shadows, Irena Praitis (2012)
In the Lake of Your Bones, Peggy Dobreer (2012)
I Was Building Up to Something, Susan Davis (2011)
Hopeless Cases, Michael Kramer (2011)
One World, Gail Newman (2011)
What We Ache For, Eric Morago (2010)
Now and Then, Lee Mallory (2009)
Pop Art: An Anthology of Southern California Poetry (2009)
In the Heaven of Never Before, Carine Topal (2008)
A Wild Region, Kate Buckley (2008)
Carving in Bone: An Anthology of Orange County Poetry (2007)
Kindness from a Dark God, Ben Trigg (2007)
A Thin Strand of Lights, Ricki Mandeville (2006)
Sleepyhead Assassins, Mindy Nettifee (2006)
Tide Pools: An Anthology of Orange County Poetry (2006)
Lost American Nights: Lyrics & Poems, Michael Ubaldini (2006)

Patrons

Moon Tide Press would like to thank the following people for their support in helping publish the finest poetry from the Southern California region. To sign up as a patron, visit www.moontidepress.com or send an email to publisher@moontidepress.com.

Anonymous
Robin Axworthy
Conner Brenner
Nicole Connolly
Bill Cushing
Susan Davis
Kristen Baum DeBeasi
Peggy Dobreer
Kate Gale
Dennis Gowans
Alexis Rhone Fancher
HanaLena Fennel
Half Off Books & Brad T. Cox
Donna Hilbert
Jim & Vicky Hoggatt
Michael Kramer
Ron Koertge & Bianca Richards
Gary Jacobelly
Ray & Christi Lacoste
Jeff Lewis
Zachary & Tammy Locklin
Lincoln McElwee
David McIntire
José Enrique Medina
Michael Miller & Rachanee Srisavasdi
Michelle & Robert Miller
Ronny & Richard Morago
Terri Niccum
Andrew November
Jeremy Ra
Luke & Mia Salazar
Jennifer Smith
Roger Sponder
Andrew Turner
Rex Wilder
Mariano Zaro
Wes Bryan Zwick